INTERMITTENT
FASTING
THE COMPLETE
KETOFAST
SOLUTION

CookNation

INTERMITTENT FASTING THE COMPLETE KETOFAST SOLUTION

THE KETOGENIC DIET COOKBOOK GUIDE TO HELP UNLOCK YOUR WEIGHT LOSS, REVERSE DISEASE & ILLNESS

DISCLAIMER

CONTENTS

KETOFAST DINNERS

KETOFAST SOUPS & SALADS

KETOFAST SAUCES & SEASONING

KETOFAST DESSERTS, SNACKS & SMOOTHIES

INTRODUCTION

Intermittent fasting combined with a ketogenic approach to living can yield previously unachievable results in weight loss, well-being and relieving the symptoms of, and sometimes even reversing, disease and illness.

PRACTICE OF KETOSIS AND INTERMITTENT FASTING

If you are reading this book it's likely you want to learn what ketosis and intermittent fasting really means and are no doubt interested in the many potential health benefits which can include weight loss and diabetes management.

Lets start by explaining what Ketosis actually is.

WHAT IS KETOSIS? HOW DOES IT AFFECT THE BODY?

The body typically gets its energy from carbohydrates through a process called glycolysis. If the body does not have carbohydrates to use, another metabolic process kicks in. This metabolic process is called ketosis(1).

Ketosis is a metabolic state/process where the body burns fat at a high rate, converting fatty acids into ketones(1). It is a normal metabolic process. When the body does not have enough glucose for energy, it burns stored fats instead; this results in a build-up of acids called ketones within the body. Ketosis describes a condition where fat stores are broken down to produce energy, which also produces ketones, a type of acid. This aids weight loss as it forces the body to burn fat stores.

In recent times nutritionists have become increasingly concerned with the intake of too much fat. The first Dietary Guidelines for Americans, published in 1980, listed, *"Avoid too much fat, saturated fat, and cholesterol"* (3). Likewise, in the UK, the NHS publication titled *"Fat: the facts"* advises against the intake of too much fat. The publication quoted *"Too much fat in your diet, especially saturated fats, can raise your cholesterol, which increases the risk of heart disease. Current UK government guidelines advise cutting down on all fats and replacing saturated fat with some unsaturated fat."*(4)

This advice however doesn't differentiate strongly enough between good/unsaturated fats and bad/saturated fats. Consuming good fats can actually help our metabolic system and is a key component in the success of the Keto Diet.

The body can be forced to enter a state of ketosis through the consumption of ketogenic low-carbohydrate diets especially to lose weight. The key principles of the ketogenic approach to eating are based on the **Atkins Diet** and the **Paleo Diet**.

The Atkins Diet is a low-carb diet, usually recommended for weight loss. This diet has evolved since its introduction in 1972 by a physician, Dr Robert C. Atkins in his best-selling book "Dr Atkins' Diet Revolution". It encourages losing weight by eating low-carbohydrate (low-carb) diets that contain proteins, vegetables, and healthy fats.

The Paleo Diet popularised by Loren Cordain, PhD is literally based on the idea that if we eat like our prehistoric ancestors, we will be leaner and less likely to get diabetes, heart disease, cancer, and other health problems. It promotes consumption of high-protein and high-fibre promising the loss of weight without rigorous calorie counting. It is these two principles that form the basis of the Ketogenic Diet (or Keto Diet). Put simply the Keto Diet is a low-carb, high-fat diet. In this diet, carbohydrate intake is significantly replaced with fat.

Various research has revealed that Ketogenic diets can cause a massive reduction in weight, cardiovascular disease and diabetes(5). Calories are derived from three major compositions fats, proteins, and carbohydrates (or carbs). Fats composition is the highest (usually more than 50 per cent), followed by protein and carbs are the lowest usually below 10 per cent of the composition. The reason for high consumption of fats is to force the body to source energy from fats instead of carbohydrate. Protein is also consumed in significant quantities to avoid the loss of muscle mass and at the same time facilitate the loss of body mass(5).

There are different classification of ketogenic diets depending on the result you are trying to achieve.

The Standard Ketogenic Diet (SKD) contains high-fat (75%), moderate-protein (20%) and very low-carb (5%). It is the most used Keto diet plan and very effective in reducing weight (2).

The Targeted Ketogenic Diet (TKD) is dubbed a Traditional Approach. It is usually combined with exercise to lose weights. Carbs are eaten 30-60 minutes prior exercise. It's advisable to choose easily digestible carbs with high Glycemic Index ranking to avoid stomach upset. The carbs consumed before exercise are assumed to burn out during exercise.

Cyclic Ketogenic Diet (CKD) involves periods of higher-carb refeeds, such as eating low-carb diets for 5 days and high-carb diets for two days.

High-protein ketogenic Diet (HPKD) is similar to SKD but contains more protein. The composition is usually 60% fat, 35% protein and 5% carbs.

Restricted Ketogenic Diet (RKD) are special Keto diets for therapeutic treatment of diseases like cancer. The carb intake is restricted below 20 grams per day(6).

Ketogenic diets do not have to be unpalatable. As with our recipes, they can include different delicious, tasty, versatile and nutritious foods that allows you to maintain your low-carb goal daily(7).

The best tasting and most effective Keto meals should include some of the following;

· Fish and seafood	· High-fat sauces	· Meat and poultry	· Olives and olive oil
· Low-carb vegetables	· Nuts and seeds	· Eggs	· Coconut oil
· Meats	· Cheese	· Plain Greek yogurt	· Butter and cream
· Natural fat	· Avocados	& cottage cheese	· Dark chocolate

These foods offer numerous health benefits such as reduced risk of diseases, improved mental health and eye health, anti-ageing benefits and maintenance of body mass(8,9,10).

High-carb foods which should be avoided include:

- Sugar
- Starch
- Beer
- Margarine
- Sugary alcoholic drinks
- Processed foods
- Grains
- Milk
- Farm-processed meats
- Artificial sweeteners
- Legumes except peanuts
- Soy products
- Tropical fruits
- High-carb fruits

INTERMITTENT FASTING:

For optimal results from Keto diets, it is logical to combine it with Intermittent Fasting (IF).

What is Intermittent Fasting?

Intermittent fasting is a pattern of eating. It is not focused on dietary restriction, instead, it is a timeline of when you eat. Just like Keto Diets, IF kicks the body into ketosis a process whereby the body breaks down fat for energy. It should not be compared to starvation. Starvation is involuntary, while IF is voluntary. A concern some people have is the fact that this method may involve skipping breakfast which many consider the most important meal of the day. However studies have shown that short-term repeated fasting in mice increased lifespan(11).

There are 6 major types of Intermittent Fasting. All of them can be successful but the best choice for you will depend on the type of result you desire and how the fasting schedule fits in which your lifestyle.

16/8 Method

This IF method, just as its name implies, involves a daily fasting of 14-16 hours with a restricted eating timeframe of 8-10 hours. Following this method of fasting can actually be as simple as not eating anything after lunch and skipping breakfast. If for example, you finished your last meal at 2pm you are not expected to eat another meal until after 6am the next day. It is acceptable for women to only fast 14-15 hours since they can respond better with shorter fasting hours(12).

5:2 Diet

This IF method was popularised by British journalist and doctor, Michael Mosley. It involves eating normally for 5 days of the week and reducing intake on two days of the same week. On the fasting days, it is recommended that women consume 500 calories, and men 600 calories. Although there has been no scientific research on the use of this method so far, there have been many studies confirming the benefits of intermittent fasting(12).

Eat-Stop-Eat

The Eat-Stop-Eat proposes 24-hour fasting once or twice in a week. You may decide to commence your fasting after breakfast, lunch, or dinner. For example if you started fasting at lunch, you will complete the 24-hour at lunch the next day.

Alternate-Day Fasting

This fasting method involves fasting for every other day. It requires enormous will power and is not recommended for anyone trying IF for the first time.

The Warrior Diet

After a long day fasting or low carb consumption, you are allowed to eat a huge meal at night. You will eat small amounts of raw fruits and vegetables during the day, then 'feast;' at night(12).

Spontaneous Meal Skipping

Skip meals occasionally, when you don't feel hungry or are too busy to cook and eat. Our bodies are well equipped to handle missing one or two meals from time to time. Just be sure to eat healthy balanced food groups in the meals you do have.

Please note that the approach to intermittent fasting is a personal one and we do not recommend one approach over another. Some methods are considered more 'extereme' than others. We recommend prior to emabarking on any diet that you seek the advice of a health professional .

To help make Intermittent Fasting more tolerable there are some drinks you could occasionally consume during the fasting period to help you remain well and active during the period:

Liquids

- Water should be top of your list whilst fasting. It's important to stay hydrated.
- Herbal teas; these taste great and can help stave off hunger. Some also have useful detoxifying benefits.
- Coffee (ideally black); drinking coffee helps suppress hunger and the caffeine it contains can also provide an energy boost. Don't drink too much though. Two cups a day is probably the maximum.
- Cider vinegar; This is a great ingredient which can be added to sparkling water to make a refreshing drink. Although it is acidic it actually helps to balance your body's pH levels. It contains almost no calories and is perfect for fasting as it helps keep your electrolytes in check and prevent deficiencies.

Food

What you can eat during fasting depends on the type of fasting you are undertaking. Some methods like 5:2 term fasting as an intake of 500/600 calories or less per day whilst other forms of IF may mean short periods of absolutely no food at all. If however you are taking in some food during IF the best sources of energy include: Low carb veg, whole grains, healthy fats (avocados and nuts), and small amounts of meat and dairy.

To maximise your weight loss program, it makes sense to combine KETO & IF. It's like effectively having two solutions to one problem. If however your health will not allow you to fast, stick solely to Keto foods.

Our delcious and easy to follow collection of high protein, high-fat, low-carb breakfasts, lunches, dinners, smoothies and snacks will help you adopt a new and exciting approach to dieting with results you'll be proud of.

Notes
- All nutritional measurements are approximate, you can use your trusted recipe measurement method.
- Carbs represent total carbs, sections where net carbs are included are tagged "net carbs"

References

1. Medical News Today. (2017). Ketosis: What is ketosis?. Available at *https://www.medicalnewstoday.com/articles/180858.php*
2. Freeman JM, Kossoff EH, Hartman AL. (2017). The ketogenic diet: one decade later. US National Library of Medicine National Institutes of Health, PMID: 17332207 DOI: 10.1542/peds.2006-2447 Available at *https://www.ncbi.nlm.nih.gov/pubmed/17332207*
3. U.S. Department of Health and Human Services and U.S. Department of Agriculture. (1980). Nutrition and Your Health: Dietary Guidelines for Americans. 1st Edition. Available at *https://health.gov/dietaryguidelines/1980thin.pdf*
4. National Health Service. (2018). Fat: the facts. Available at *https://www.nhs.uk/live-well/eat-well/different-fats-nutrition/*
5. Bueno NB, de Melo IS, de Oliveira SL, da Rocha Ataide T. (2013). Very-low-carbohydrate ketogenic diet v. low-fat diet for long-term weight loss: a meta-analysis of randomised controlled trials. US National Library of Medicine National Institutes of Health, 110(7):1178-87. doi: 10.1017/S0007114513000548. Available at *https://www.ncbi.nlm.nih.gov/pubmed/23651522*
6. Giulio Z, Norina M, Anna P, Franco S, Salvatore V, et al. (2010). Metabolic management of glioblastoma multiforme using standard therapy together with a restricted ketogenic diet: Case Report. US National Library of Medicine National Institutes of Health, doi: 10.1186/1743-7075-7-33.
7. Franziska S. 2017. 16 Foods to Eat on a Ketogenic Diet. HealthLine. Available at *https://www.healthline.com/nutrition/ketogenic-diet-foods#section1*
8. Morris MC, Evans DA, Tangney CC, Bienias JL, Wilson RS. Fish consumption and cognitive decline with age in a large community study. US National Library of Medicine National Institutes of Health. 88(6):1618-25. doi: 10.3945/ajcn.2007.25816.
9. Andreas E. 2018. Ketogenic diet foods – what to eat. Diet Doctor. Available at *https://www.dietdoctor.com/low-carb/keto/foods*
10. Martina S. 2015. Complete Keto Diet Food List: What to Eat and Avoid on a Low-Carb Diet. Ketodiet. Available at *https://ketodietapp.com/Blog/lchf/Keto-Diet-Food-List-What-to-Eat-and-Avoid*
11. Sogawa H, Kubo C (2000). Influence of short-term repeated fasting on the longevity of female (NZB x NZW) F1 mice. US National Library of Medicine National Institutes of Health, PMID: 10854629.
12. Kris G (2017). 6 Popular Ways to Do Intermittent Fasting. Health Line. Available at *https://www.healthline.com/nutrition/6-ways-to-do-intermittent-fasting#section1*

ABOUT 🍎 CookNation

CookNation is the leading publisher of innovative and practical recipe books for the modern, health conscious cook.

CookNation titles bring together delicious, easy and practical recipes with their unique no nonsense approach - making cooking for diets and healthy eating fast, simple and fun. With a range of #1 best-selling titles - from the innovative 'Skinny' calorie-counted series, to the 5:2 Diet Recipes collection - CookNation recipe books prove that 'Diet' can still mean 'Delicious'!

To browse all CookNation's recipe books visit **www.bellmackenzie.com**

BREAKFASTS

KETO CINNAMON ROLLS

calories: 320
fat: 29g
carbs: 5g
fibre: 0g
protein: 11g

Ingredients

For the dough:
- 12½oz/360g almond flour
- 12½oz/360g mozzarella
- 3oz/75g cream cheese
- ½ tsp cinnamon (more to taste)
- 1 egg, whisked

- 2 squeezes of liquid stevia (more to taste)

For the filling:
- 3 tbsp melted butter
- 2 tsp cinnamon
- Icing:

- 4 tbsp cream cheese
- 2 tbsp vanilla extract
- 2oz/60ml butter at room temperature
- 1 tbsp lemon juice
- 3 squeezes of liquid stevia

Method

1 Preheat oven to 200C/400F/GAS6.

2 In a bowl, add mozzarella and cream cheese. Put in the microwave for one minute, take out and stir.

3 Put in the microwave for another minute, stir again.

4 Add in the almond flour, stevia, cinnamon and the egg. Mix to combine well.

5 The dough will be a little wet but if it's too wet that you can't get it to stop sticking to your fingers then add a little more almond flour.

6 Roll the dough out flat with a rolling pin or with a piece of plastic wrap on top and use a wine bottle.

7 Once you've rolled it out, spread on the melted butter and sprinkle on the cinnamon.

8 Roll it up long ways until you have a long cylinder. Use a knife or pizza cutter and cut into pieces. Place these on a baking sheet lined with parchment paper.

9 Bake at 200C/400F/GAS 6 for 10-12 mins.

10 While they're baking, make the icing. You can do this with a mixer. Add cream cheese and butter and mix until creamy. Add in the vanilla extract and lemon juice. Mix until well combined.

11 Once cinnamon rolls are done, put on icing. If you put it on immediately, it will melt a little into the actual cinnamon roll. Instead allow the rolls to cool for ten minutes before spreading over the top.

INDIAN BREAKFAST DISH

calories: 252
fat: 21g
carbs: 8g
fibre: 4g
protein: 7g

Ingredients

- 1 head cauliflower
- 2 tbsp olive oil
- 1 tbsp yellow mustard seeds
- 1 tbsp cumin seeds
- 1 red onion, chopped
- 5 curry leaves
- 1 tsp fresh grated ginger
- 1 green chilli pepper
- 10 peanuts, chopped
- Fresh Coriander, for garnish

Method

1 Break cauliflower into large florets. Transfer into a food processor and pulse until completely broken down into couscous-sized pieces.

2 Heat the olive oil in a frying pan and add the mustard seeds and cumin.

3 Once they start to sizzle, add chopped onion, curry leaves, ginger, green chillies and peanuts.

4 Fry on low-medium heat until the onions get translucent.

5 Salt to taste.

6 Add the couscous-sized cauliflower, combine well and fry for a few minutes.

7 Add a little water so it almost covers the mixture.

Cook for 10 mins with the lid on.

8 Keep checking and stirring every few minutes to ensure that nothing sticks to the bottom of the pan.

9 Cook until the water evaporates.

10 Finish with adding the fresh Coriander.

CHEF'S NOTE
You can replace the olive oil with ghee or butter.

KETO MEXICAN SCRAMBLED EGGS

calories: 229
fat: 18g
carbs: 2g
fibre: 1g
protein: 14g

Ingredients

- 6 eggs
- 3 spring onions
- 2 pickled jalapeños
- 1 tomato
- 3oz/75g grated cheese
- 2 tbsp butter, for frying
- Salt and pepper

Method

1 Finely chop the spring onions, jalapeños and tomatoes.

2 Fry in butter for 3 minutes on medium heat.

3 Beat the eggs and pour into the frying pan. Scramble for 2 minutes.

4 Add cheese and season to serve.

CHEF'S NOTE

You can also serve with avocado and shredded crisp lettuce.

NO-BREAD KETO SANDWICH

calories: 334
fat: 20g
carbs: 2g
fibre: 0g
protein: 20g

Ingredients

- 2 tsp butter
- 4 eggs
- 4 slices smoked ham slices
- 2oz/50g cheddar cheese or provolone cheese, cut in thick slices
- Salt and pepper

Method

1 Add butter to a frying pan and place over medium heat.

2 Add eggs and fry. until the yolk is firm

3 Add salt and pepper to taste.

4 Use two of the fried eggs as the base for each sandwich.

5 Place the ham slices on each base and then add the cheese to the bases.

6 Top off each base with the other fried eggs. Leave in the pan, on low heat and allow the cheese to melt before serving.

CHEF'S NOTE
Sprinkle a few drops of Tabasco or Worcestershire sauce if you're in the mood, and serve immediately.

KETO WAFFLES

calories: 280
fat: 26g
carbs: 4.5g
fibre: 2g
protein: 7g

Ingredients

- 5 eggs
- 4 tbsp coconut flour
- 4 tbsp granulated sweetener
- 1 tsp baking powder

- 2 tsp vanilla
- 3 tbsp full fat milk or cream
- 125g/4oz butter melted

Method

1 Prepare two bowls.

2 In first bowl: Whisk the egg whites until firm and form stiff peaks.

3 In second bowl: Mix the egg yolks, coconut flour, sweetener, and baking powder.

4 Add the melted butter to the egg yolks slowly mixing to ensure it is a smooth consistency.

5 Then add the milk and vanilla to the yolks and mix well.

6 Gently fold spoons of the whisked egg whites into the yolk mixture. Try to keep as much of the air and fluffiness as possible.

7 Place enough of the waffle mixture into the warm waffle maker to make one waffle. Cook until golden.

8 Repeat until all the mixture has been used.

CHEF'S NOTE

The waffles be frozen in between sheets of baking paper placed inside an airtight container.

BLUEBERRY COCONUT PORRIDGE

calories: 405
fat: 34g
carbs: 8g
fibre: 7g
protein: 10g

Ingredients

- 250ml/1 cup almond milk
- 2oz/50g ground flaxseed
- 2oz/50g coconut flour
- 1 tsp cinnamon
- 1 tsp vanilla extract
- 10 drops liquid stevia

- 1 pinch salt

Toppings
- 2 tbsp butter
- 75g/3oz blueberries
- 2 tbsp pumpkin seeds
- 1oz/25g shaved coconut

Method

1 Gently warm the almond milk in a pan on a low flame.

2 Add in flaxseed, coconut flour, cinnamon and sal, using a whisk to break up any clumps.

3 Heat until slightly bubbling. Add in liquid stevia and vanilla extract.

4 When the mixture is as thick as you want it to be,

5 Remove from the heat and add in the toppings: butter, blueberries, pumpkin seeds and shaved coconut!

CHEF'S NOTE
If you want additional fat and protein slowly add a beaten egg into the cooking porridge.

LOW-CARB PUMPKIN & MUSHROOM RISOTTO

calories: 312
fat: 24g
carbs: 10g
fibre: 4g
protein: 12.9g

Ingredients

- 14oz/400g pumpkin
- 2 tbsp extra virgin olive oil
- 800ml chicken or vegetable stock (about 3 ½ cups)
- 2 garlic cloves, crushed
- 1 onion

- 2 heads cauliflower
- 5oz/150g mushrooms, sliced
- 1 tbsp butter
- 3 tbsp cream
- 6 sprigs of fresh thyme
- ¼ tsp sea salt, or to taste

- ¼ tsp cracked black pepper
- 2oz/50g pumpkin seeds
- 2oz/50g grated parmesan cheese

Method

1 Preheat oven to 190C/375F/GAS5. Peel the pumpkin, remove the seeds and chop into small chunks (¾ inch). Place on a baking tray and toss with 1 tbsp of the oil and a pinch of salt. Roast in the oven for 20 minutes until soft.

2 Add the stock to a pot and simmer on a medium heat until the volume reduces to about 500 ml (this concentrates the stock and really adds to the flavour.)

3 Whizz the cauliflower in a high-speed food processor until it resembles a rice consistency.

4 Peel and finely dice the onion. Fry the onion in the rest of the olive oil on a medium heat for a few minutes until translucent. Add the garlic and cauliflower rice and fry for a further 2-3 minutes.

5 Add the stock, salt, pepper, thyme and simmer on a medium heat until all the stock is absorbed.

6 Place the seeds on a baking tray and roast in the oven for 5-6 minutes until golden. Remove from the oven and allow to cool.

7 Heat the butter in a pan and fry the mushrooms on a medium heat for 2-3 minutes.

8 Stir through the mushrooms, cream, pumpkin and half of the cheese. Taste and add more seasoning if required.

9 Spoon the Pumpkin, Mushroom and Thyme Cauliflower Rice Risotto into bowls and top with pumpkin seeds, the remaining cheese and a sprinkling of fresh thyme leaves.

KETO MORNING HOT POCKETS

calories: 455
fat: 38g
carbs: 5g
fibre: 2g
protein: 25g

Ingredients

- 7oz/200g mozzarella
- 2½oz/60g almond flour
- 2 eggs

- 2 tbsp unsalted butter
- 4 slices streaky bacon cooked

Method

1 Preheat the oven to 200C/400F/GAS6

2 On a gentle heat melt the mozzarella & add the almond flour. Stir until well-combined into a soft dough and remove from the heat.

3 Roll the dough out thinly to approx 15cm square between 2 sheets of parchment paper.

4 Quickly scramble the eggs in a frying pan in melted butter and lay them with streaky streaky bacon slices along the centre of the dough.

5 Fold over and seal the dough. Add some holes on the dough surface using a fork. This helps release the steam while baking.

6 Bake for about 20 mins or until it turns golden brown and firm to the touch. Remove from oven and enjoy!

CHEF'S NOTE

One ounce of mozzarella has 183 milligrams of calcium, which is over 18 per cent of the recommended daily intake.

CHEWY MUESLI BAR

calories: 180
fat: 17g
carbs: 2g
fibre: 0.5g
protein: 4g

Ingredients

- 12½oz/360g sliced almonds
- 4oz/125g flaked coconut (unsweetened)
- 4oz/125g pecans
- 4oz/125g sunflower seeds
- 4oz/125g dried, unsweetened cranberries (chopped)
- 4oz/120ml butter
- 4oz/125g powdered erythritol
- ½ tsp vanilla extract
- 1 pinch salt

Method

1 Preheat the oven to 150C/300F/GAS2 and line a square baking dish with parchment.

2 Combine the almonds, coconut, pecans, and sunflower seeds in a food processor.

3 Pulse the mixture until it is finely chopped and crumbed..

4 Pour the mixture into a bowl and stir in the cranberries and a pinch of salt.

5 Melt the butter in a saucepan over low heat then whisk in the erythritol and vanilla extract.

6 Pour the mixture over the muesli and stir until well combined.

7 Press the mixture into the prepared dish, compacting it as much as possible, and bake for 20-25 minutes.

8 Cool the mixture in the pan completely then remove and cut into 16 bars.

CHEF'S NOTE
Pack into the dish very tightly and let cool after baking to stick properly.

ONION CHIVE CAULIFLOWER HASH BROWNS

calories: 93
fat: 6g
carbs: 4g
fibre: 2g
protein: 5g

Ingredients

- 15oz/425g riced cauliflower
- 1 egg
- ¼ tsp salt
- Couple pinches of cracked black pepper
- 1 finely diced onion
- 1 finely diced red pepper
- 2 tbsp onion & chive cottage cheese
- ½ tbsp olive oil

Method

1 In a bowl, mix the cauliflower rice, egg, salt & pepper, onions and red peppers until thoroughly combined.

2 In a small pan over medium-high heat, add olive oil.Once the pan is hot and olive oil rolls around easily in the pan, use a large spoon to scoop half the cauliflower mix into the pan.

3 Use the spoon to flatten the cauliflower down to about ⅓ inch thick, and also to smooth around the side so that it's in a round or rectangle shape.

4 Let sit and cook until brown and crispy underneath, about 4-5 minutes.

5 Use a spatula to flip the hash brown.

6 Let the hash brown cook until crispy underneath (another 3-4 minutes)

7 Remove from your pan with a spatula, and repeat with the second half of the "batter".

8 pile a tablespoon of ottage cheesd on top to serve.

CHEF'S NOTE
Calcium and vitamin D found in cottage cheese reduces the risk of breast cancer.

23

CHEESY SCRAMBLED EGGS

calories: 353
fat: 33g
carbs: 1.2g
fibre: 1g
protein: 19g

Ingredients

- 2 eggs
- 1 tbsp butter
- 1oz/25g cheddar cheese

- 2 tbsp chopped chives
- 1 red pepper, sliced

Method

1 Heat a frying pan on the stove, adding the butter and saute the peppers for a few minutes untl softened.

2 Crack the eggs into the pan and add the chives..

3 Let the eggs cook cook and move them arounf the pan until just about to set.

4 Add the cheese and and serve.

CHEF'S NOTE
Cheddar cheese contain vitamin A which is essential for proper functioning of organs, good vision and cell growth.

CHEESY FRITTATA MUFFINS

calories: 205
fat: 16.1g
carbs: 1.3g
fibre: 0g
protein: 13.6g

Ingredients

- 8 eggs
- 120ml/ ½ cup cream
- 4oz/125g streaky bacon, pre-cooked and chopped
- 4oz/125g cheddar cheese
- 1 tbsp butter
- 2 tsp dried parsley
- ½ tsp pepper
- ¼ tsp salt

Method

1 Preheat the oven to 190C/375F/GAS5.

2 Whisk the eggs and cream in a bowl.

3 Fold in the streaky bacon, cheese, and oter ingredients.

4 Grease a muffin tin with butter.

5 Pour the mixture, filling each cup about ¾ way.

6 Place in the oven for 15-18 minutes, or until puffy and golden on the edges.

7 Remove from the oven and let cool for 1 minute.

CHEF'S NOTE
Use whichever type of full fat cheese you prefer in these delicious muffins.

BAKED DENVER OMELETTE

calories: 252
fat: 15g
carbs: 4g
fibre: 2g
protein: 19g

Ingredients

- 1 chopped red pepper
- 1 chopped green pepper
- 1 onion
- 2 tsp olive oil
- 8oz/225g chopped cooked ham

- 8 eggs
- 1 tbsp milk
- Salt and freshly mince black pepper
- 4oz/125g grated cheddar cheese

Method

1 Preheat oven to 200C/400F/GAS6.

2 Grease the baking dish with a little oil. Sprinkle the ham into an even layer in bottom of baking dish.

3 Heat the oil in a frying pan over medium-high heat. Once hot, add the peppers and onion and cook until softened for about 4 minutes.

4 Evenly pour the pepper mixture over the ham then sprinkle evenly with cheese.

5 In a large mixing bowl whisk together eggs and milk until well blended. Season with salt and pepper and stir, then pour over mixture in baking dish.

6 Bake in preheated oven for approx 20 minutes until puffy and set.

7 Cut and serve warm.

CHEF'S NOTE
You can add sliced avocados, chopped chives and hot sauce for serving.

BLACKBERRY EGG BAKE

calories: 114
fat: 10g
carbs: 4g
fibre: 2g
protein: 8.5g

Ingredients

- 5 eggs
- 1 tbsp butter, melted
- 3 tbsp coconut flour
- 1 tsp grated fresh ginger
- ¼ tsp vanilla
- ⅓ tsp fine sea salt
- Zest of half an orange
- 1 tsp fresh rosemary
- 4oz/125g fresh blackberries

Method

1 Preheat oven to 180C/350F/GAS4 and grease four ramekins.

2 Place all of the ingredients except the fresh rosemary and blackberries into a blender and process about one or two minutes on high until the mixture is completely combined and smooth.

3 Add the rosemary and pulse a few times until rosemary is just combined.

4 Divide the egg mixture between the four ramekins and add blackberries to each ramekin.

5 Place the filled ramekins on a baking sheet and bake for fifteen to twenty minutes until the egg mixture puffs and is cooked through.

6 Cool on a rack a few minutes before indulging. Can be eaten in or popped out of the ramekins.

CHEF'S NOTE
You can replace orange zest with lemon zest, and add cinnamon and blueberries instead of ginger, blackberries.

27

BLUEBERRIES & CREAM CREPES

calories: 390
fat: 32g
carbs: 7g
fibre: 3g
protein: 13g

Ingredients

Crepe Batter
- 2oz/50g cream cheese
- 2 eggs
- 10 drops liquid stevia
- ¼ tsp cinnamon
- ¼ tsp baking soda
- Sea salt, to taste

Filling
- 4oz/125g cream cheese
- ½ tsp vanilla extract
- 2 tbsp erythritol
- 2½oz/60g blueberries

Method

1 Combine the cream cheese and eggs in a bowl and beat them with an electric hand mixer until completely smooth.

2 Add in the stevia, cinnamon, baking soda and sea salt. Combine that all together.

3 Heat up a medium-sized, nonstick pan on medium heat. Add in some butter or coconut oil to grease it lightly.

4 Pour in a bit of batter (about ¼ cup at a time) while swirling the pan to help it spread to the edges. Cook until the edges start to crisp up (about 3 minutes per crepe). Wiggle a spatula around the edges to loosen them, then under the crepe gently and flip.

5 While the crepes are cooking, prepare your filling by combining the filling cream cheese, vanilla extract and powdered erythritol in a bowl. Beat with an electric hand mixer until smooth and creamy.

6 When the crepes have finished cooking, add a bit of the filling down the centre of each crepe. Add some fresh blueberries and wrap it up.

CHEF'S NOTE
You can microwave the berries for 30 seconds to soften.

STREAKY BACON, EGG & CHEESE CUPS

calories: 201
fat: 14g
carbs: 2g
fibre: 0g
protein: 16g

Ingredients

- 12 eggs
- 4oz/125g frozen spinach, thawed and drained
- 12 strips streaky bacon
- Handful of grated cheddar cheese
- Salt and pepper, to taste

Method

1 Preheat the oven to 200C/400F/GAS6.

2 Fry the streaky bacon in a frying pan and set aside on a cooling rack to drain excess oil.

3 Grease muffin pan generously with coconut oil or olive oil then line each cup with one slice of streaky bacon.

4 Press the slice down, it will stick up on either side (these are your handles!)

5 In a large bowl, crack and lightly beat eggs.

6 Wring out any extra water from the spinach beforehand with a clean kitchen towel or paper towel. Stir the spinach into the eggs,

7 Scoop egg mixture into each muffin well, filling them up about ¾ of the way.

8 Sprinkle the tops evenly with the shredded cheese and season with salt and pepper.

9 Bake on the middle rack for 15 minutes.

CHEF'S NOTE
Store in an airtight container in the refrigerator. Heat up in a microwave for better taste.

BRIE & APPLE CREPES

calories: 411
fat: 37g
carbs: 6g
fibre: 2g
protein: 14g

Ingredients

Crepe Batter
- 4oz/125g cream cheese
- 4 eggs
- ½ tsp baking soda
- ¼ tsp sea salt

Toppings
- 2oz/50g chopped pecans
- 1 tbsp unsalted butter
- ¼ tsp cinnamon
- 1 gala apple
- 4oz/125g brie cheese
- Fresh mint leaves, for garnish

Method

1 Begin by combining the batter ingredients in a Nutribullet or blender. Blend until smooth.

2 Heat up a small amount of unsalted butter in a non-stick pan on medium heat.

3 Ladle some of the crepe batter into the pan and swirl the contents around so that the batter is thin and spread out evenly.

4 Let cook until the top looks dry (about 2-3 minutes), then flip gently with a large spatula and cook the other side for a few seconds.

5 Repeat this step until you have about 8 crepes. Layer them on top of each other on a plate while you prep the toppings/fillings.

6 Melt a tbsp of butter in a small pan and toast the chopped pecans until fragrant. Sprinkle with cinnamon and mix. Then, transfer them to a plate to cool.

7 Slice the apple & brie thinly. .Arrange the apple slices and brie on 1 crepe and top with some of the toasted pecans. Repeat for all the crepes until all the toppings have been used.

8 Garnish with mint and enjoy with a fork and knife or rolled up

CHEF'S NOTE
You can roll each crepe into delicious little cigars and pack away for lunch later. You can also store in a refrigerator.

HAM & CHEESE WAFFLES

calories: 626
fat: 48g
carbs: 5g
fibre: 3.2g
protein: 45g

Ingredients

- 4 eggs
- 2½oz/60g unflavored whey protein powder
- 1 tsp baking powder
- 6 tbsp melted butter
- ½ tsp sea salt
- 2 slices ham, chopped
- Handful of cheddar cheese, grated
- A few pinches of paprika
- 1 tbsp fresh basil

Method

1 Start by separating eggs into two mixing bowls. Into the bowl with the egg yolks, add the protein powder, baking powder, melted butter and sea salt. Whisk to combine.

2 Add the finely chopped ham and grated cheddar cheese to the egg yolk mixture and carefully fold.

3 Whisk the egg whites and a pinch of salt with an electric hand mixer until stiff peaks form. Gently fold in half the stiff egg whites into the egg yolk mixture. Try not to let the egg yolk deflate. Fold in the other half once the egg yolks have aerated a bit.

4 Add ¼ cup of batter to a well-greased waffle maker and cook on medium heat for about 3-4 minutes each. (or according to manufacturer's instructions.

5 Cook only until they're lightly golden. The residual heat will continue to cook the waffle even once it's out of the waffle maker.

6 Sprinkle with a little paprika and fresh basil.

CHEF'S NOTE
Paprika contains vitamin E which helps control blood clot formation and promotes healthy blood vessel function.

THE PERFECT SCRAMBLE

calories: 444
fat: 35g
carbs: 9g
fibre: 4g
protein: 25g

Ingredients

- 6 eggs
- 2 tbsp butter
- 2 tbsp sour cream
- 2 stalk green onion
- 4 strips streaky bacon

- ½ tsp salt
- ½ tsp garlic powder
- ½ tsp onion powder
- ¼ tsp black pepper
- ¼ tsp paprika

Method

1 Crack the eggs into a cold, ungreased pan and add the butter. Only start mixing the eggs once they're on the heat. This ensures no areas of the egg starts to cook before the others. We are saving the seasoning for after the eggs are cooked. Adding salt will only break the eggs down and create a watery finish; we want creamy!

2 Place the pan on a medium-high heat and begin stirring the eggs and butter together with a silicone spatula. As the butter melts slowly, it'll give the eggs extra creaminess and will also prevent the eggs from sticking to the pan.

3 While stirring the eggs, let some streaky bacon strips cook to your desired crispiness in another pan (or bake them!).

4 Alternate stirring the eggs on the heat and off the heat. If you see the eggs starting to cook in a thin, dry layer at the bottom of the pan, take it off the heat! Scrape it with your silicone spatula and that layer should integrate back with the rest of the eggs and regain some creaminess.

5 Stir alternatively on and off the flame a few seconds on the flame, a few seconds off.

6 The eggs should start coming together slowly. When they're almost done cooking to your liking, turn the flame off. The eggs will continue cooking a little more from the residual heat from the pan.

7 Add sour cream, salt and paprika to serve.

8 To add some contrasting flavor, add stalks of srping onions, chopped.

SHAKSHUKA

calories: 490
fat: 39g
carbs: 4g
fibre: 3g
protein: 35g

Ingredients

- 250ml/1 cup marinara sauce
- 1 chilli pepper
- 4 eggs
- 1oz/25g feta cheese
- Pinch of ground cumin
- Salt and pepper, to taste
- Fresh basil

Method

1 Preheat the oven to 200C/400F/GAS6.

2 Heat a small frying pan on a medium flame with a cup of marinara sauce and some chopped chilli pepper. Let the chilli pepper cook for about 5 minutes in the sauce.

3 Crack and gently lower your eggs into the marinara sauce.

4 Sprinkle feta cheese all over the eggs and season with salt, pepper and cumin.

5 Using an oven mitt, place the frying pan into your oven and bake for about 10 minutes. Now the frying pan should be hot enough to continue cooking the food in the oven instead of heating itself up first.

6 Once the eggs are cooked, but still runny, take the frying pan out with an oven mitt. Chop some fresh basil and sprinkle over the shakshuka.

CHEF'S NOTE

You can make your sauce from scratch instead of using marinara sauce if you have the time.

LUNCHES

BLT CHICKEN SALAD STUFFED AVOCADOS

calories: 291
fat: 23g
carbs: 13g
fibre: 6g
protein: 25g

Ingredients

- 12 slices of streaky bacon
- 12½oz/360g shredded roasted/rotisserie chicken
- 2 large roma tomatoes, chopped
- 14oz/400g cottage cheese
- 2 shredded Romaine lettuce
- 3 avocados

Method

1 Preheat your oven to 200C/400F/GAS 6

2 Lay the streaky bacon out on a foil lined baking sheet

3 Bake for 10 minutes and, when cooked, lay the streaky bacon out over several sheets of paper towels to cool before crumbling.

4 In a large bowl, combine the chicken, cottage cheese, lettuce , tomatoes, crumbled streaky bacon, and mix together

5 Season to taste with salt and pepper

6 Half your avocados, remove the pits, and season lightly with salt and pepper.

7 Pile the the chicken salad over the top of of each avocado half to serve.

CHEF'S NOTE
The recipe is gluten free.

VEGETARIAN KETO CLUB SALAD

calories: 330
fat: 26g
carbs: 5g
fibre: 2g
protein: 17g

Ingredients

- 2 tbsp sour cream
- 2 tbsp mayonnaise
- ½ tbsp garlic powder
- ½ tbsp onion powder
- ½ tbsp dried parsley
- 1 tbsp milk

- 3 boiled eggs, sliced
- 4oz/125g cheddar cheese, cubed
- 2 Romaine lettuce, shredded
- 4oz/125g cherry tomatoes, halved
- 1 cucumber, diced
- 1 tbsp dijon mustard

Method

1 Mix the sour cream, mayonnaise, and dried herbs together until combined.

2 Add one tbsp of milk and mix to make a dressing..

3 Layer your salad with the salad vegetables, cheese, and sliced egg. Add a spoonful of Dijon mustard in the centre.

4 Drizzle with the prepared dressing, about 2 tbsps for one serving, then toss to coat.

CHEF'S NOTE
Cucumber contains antioxidants which prevent the accumulation of harmful free radicals reducing the risk of chronic disease.

KETO BAKED GARLIC PARMESAN SALMON

calories: 318
fat: 24g
carbs: 1g
fibre: 0.3g
protein: 25g

Ingredients

- 1lb/453g wild caught salmon fillet (preferably frozen)
- 2 tbsp butter (pasture raised, grass fed)
- 2 cloves garlic, minced or pressed
- 2oz/50g parmesan cheese, grated
- 2oz/50g mayonnaise (made with avocado oil)
- 2 tbsp organic dried parsley
- Sea salt and pepper

Method

1 Preheat oven to 180C/350F/GAS4 and line baking pan with parchment paper.

2 Place salmon on a baking tray and lightly season with sea salt and pepper. Set aside while preparing the topping.

3 In a medium-sized frying pan, melt butter and lightly saute garlic over medium heat. Once the garlic has softened, reduce the heat to low and add in the remaining ingredients, stirring until combined and melted.

4 Spread this mixture over the salmon fillets, place in the oven and bake for 10-15 minutes or until cooked through.

5 Check salmon with a fork. Don't overcook to remain slightly translucent.

CHEF'S NOTE

Sea salt provides the body with minerals like zinc, iron and potassium which helps prevent your body from "keto flu" majorly caused by electrolyte deficiencies.

KETO BEEF STUFFED PEPPERS

calories: 410
fat: 31g
carbs: 11g
fibre: 3g
protein: 21g

Ingredients

- 1 tbsp of olive oil
- 2 slices streaky bacon, finely chopped
- 1 onion, peeled and finely chopped
- 15 white button mushrooms, finely chopped

- 11oz/300g minced beef
- 1 tbsp smoked paprika
- 3 large sweet peppers
- Salt and freshly mince black pepper, to taste

Method

1 Preheat the oven to 180C/350F/GAS4.

2 Cut the top off the peppers and remove all seeds. Lightly brush olive oil on the entire pepper, inside and out. Set aside.

3 Heat the olive oil in a pan. Cook the streaky bacon until crispy. Remove streaky bacon, keeping as much oil in the pan as possible.

4 Add the onions and mushrooms to the oil and cook until soft. Then add the beef and paprika. Cook until the beef is browned. Season with salt and pepper. Remove from heat.

5 Scoop the beef and mushroom mixture into the peppers.

6 Place the peppers on a baking tray and bake for 20-25 minutes.

7 Garnish with chopped parsley.

CHEF'S NOTE

You can also enjoy with a batch of keto hummus and some veg sticks.

KETO EASY TACO BOWLS WITH CAULIFLOWER RICE

calories: 459
fat: 38g
carbs: 9g
fibre: 3g
protein: 21g

Ingredients

For taco bowl
- 450g/1lb of minced beef
- 3 cloves of garlic, minced or finely diced
- 1 onion, finely diced
- 6 cherry tomatoes, finely diced

- 1 pepper, diced
- 1 tsp of fresh ginger, grated
- 2 tsp of cumin powder
- Dash of chilli powder, to taste
- 2 tbsp avocado oil
- Salt and pepper, to taste

For the cauliflower rice
- 11oz/300g cauliflower rice
- 2 tbsp of coconut oil, to cook cauliflower with
- Chilli powder and salt, to taste

Method

1 In a large frying pan, heat avocado oil and garlic. Add minced beef and cook until almost completely browned.

2 Add onion, tomatoes, and pepper. Cook until vegetables are soft.

3 Add ginger, cumin, chilli powder, salt, and pepper, to taste. Mix well to combine.

4 To make the cauliflower rice, sauté the cauliflower pieces in the coconut oil on high heat for 5 mins until softened. Season with chilli powder and salt, to taste.

5 Serve taco meat over the cauliflower "rice."

CHEF'S NOTE
Cauliflower rice is made by pulsing cauliflower florets in a food processor.

KETO CURRIED TUNA SALAD

calories: 626
fat: 37g
carbs: 14g
fibre: 2.6g
protein: 47g

Ingredients

- 6oz/175g tuna, drained and flaked
- 2 tbsp mayo
- 2 tsp curry powder
- ½ red onion, sliced
- 1 tsp dried parsley
- 5 black pitted olives, sliced
- Salt and pepper, to taste

Method

1 Drain and flake the tuna in a bowl.

2 Mix with the mayo, curry powder, and dried parsley.

3 Combine with the olives and red onion.

4 Season with salt and pepper, to taste.

5 Serve with a spinach salad or cauliflower rice.

CHEF'S NOTE
Curry powder is a great 'cheat' ingredient to have in the cupboard.

41

BEANLESS PUMPKIN KETO CHILLI RECIPE

calories: 189
fat: 9g
carbs: 6g
fibre: 3g
protein: 17g

Ingredients

- 1lb/450g grass fed minced beef
- 1 onion
- 1nred pepper
- 500ml/2 cups tomato passata/sieved tomatoes

- 1¾lb/800g tomatoes, diced
- 15oz/425g pumpkin, diced
- ½ tbsp chilli powder
- 1 tsp cayenne pepper
- 1 tsp cumin

Method

1 Brown the meat in a large pan over medium heat.

2 Chop the onion and pepper, then add into the pan with the meat. Cook until the onions become translucent (3-5 minutes)

3 Add in the rest of the ingredients and let simmer on low for 30 minutes.

4 Taste your chilli, adjust seasonings as you like and cook for another 30 minutes.

CHEF'S NOTE
Tomatoes contains antioxidants that have been proven to be effective against many forms of cancer.

KETO SOUTHERN FRIED CHICKEN TENDER

calories: 365
fat: 21g
carbs: 3.5g
fibre: 4g
protein: 38.5g

Ingredients

- 4 chicken breasts
- 5oz/150g almond flour
- 1 egg
- ½ tbsp cayenne pepper
- ½ tbsp onion salt

- ½ tbsp garlic powder
- ½ tbsp dried mixed herbs
- 1 tsp salt
- 1 tsp black pepper

Method

1 Preheat the oven to 180C/350F/GAS4

2 Slice up chicken into strips, about 5-6 pieces per breast. Lay chicken strips out on a plate.

3 Mix all dry ingredients, except the almond flour to make a spice mix.

4 Using half of the spice mix, coat the chicken evenly. Turn over the chicken and coat the other side.

5 Combine the rest of the spice mix with almond flour in a bowl. In a separate bowl, whisk your egg well.

6 Take the chicken one piece at a time, and dunk it into the egg, and then dunk it straight into the almond flour mixture. Roll it around in the flour to make sure it is evenly coated.

7 Place the coated chicken on a greased baking tray.

8 Place in the oven for about 20-25 mins or until cooked through.

CHEF'S NOTE

Be careful, so that the coating doesn't stick to the rack and come away from the keto fried chicken.

BAKED STREAKY BACON COATED CHICKEN TENDERS

calories: 320
fat: 20g
carbs: 2g
fibre: 0g
protein: 29g

Ingredients

- 2 tsp salt flakes
- 2 tsp cayenne pepper
- 2 tsp paprika
- 2 tsp garlic powder
- 1 tsp onion powder

- 1 tsp oregano
- 1 tsp thyme
- 2lb/900g chicken min breast fillets
- 16 slices streaky bacon

Method

1 Preheat oven to 220C/425F/GAS7. Line a large rimmed baking tray and top with metal rack.

2 In large plastic zipper bag, dump in all the herbs and spices. Close bag and shake to blend.

3 Place each chicken tender in the zipper bag, close, and shake bag to coat the chicken in the spice blend. Once coated wrap in streaky bacon being sure to tuck in the ends and then place on rack in prepared pan.

4 Bake for 35 minutes or until cooled through. Streaky bacon should be crispy. If streaky bacon isn't crispy, you can place under the grill for a minute or two.

CHEF'S NOTE
Serve with a fresh green salad.

KETO CHICKEN BROCCOLI CASSEROLE

calories: 445
fat: 27.3g
carbs: 14g
fibre: 4.9g
protein: 39.6g

Ingredients

- 2 tbsp coconut oil divided
- 1½pint/1 litre fresh broccoli florets
- 1 onion, diced
- Sea salt
- Pepper
- 8oz/225g mushrooms sliced
- 750g/1lb 11oz cooked chicken shredded
- 9oz/250g chicken stock
- 8½oz/250ml full fat coconut milk
- 2 eggs

Method

1 Preheat the oven to 180C/350F/GAS4. Grease a casserole pan with half the coconut oil and set aside.

2 Steam the broccoli until just barely cooked and set aside, uncovered.

3 In a sauce pan melt the coconut oil, brown the onions and season with salt and pepper. Add the mushrooms, saute until cooked and move the pan off the heat.

4 Transfer the broccoli, mushroom, onions, and shredded chicken into the casserole pan distributing evenly.

5 Mix the stock, coconut milk and eggs with a pinch of salt & pepper in a bowl and pour over the contents of the casserole dish.

6 Place the casserole in the oven and cook for 35 to 40 minutes or until cooked through.

7 Remove from the oven and serve.

CHEF'S NOTE

Serve with a pile of steamed greens.

KETO CHICKEN CURRY

calories: 357
fat: 27g
carbs: 6g
fibre: 3g
protein: 22g

Ingredients

- 1lb/450g chicken or turkey mince
- 14oz/400ml coconut milk
- 1 tbsp curry powder
- ½ cauliflower head, broken into small pieces
- 2 tbsp coconut oil, to cook with
- Salt and pepper, to taste

Method

1 Add coconut oil to a small pot and cook the mince chicken until slightly browned.

2 Add coconut milk, curry powder, and salt and simmer with the lid on for 15 minutes.

3 Then add in the cauliflower and cook for another 5 minutes.

4 Season with additional salt and pepper, to taste.

CHEF'S NOTE

Curry powder increases metabolism and aids pain relief.

KETO ASIAGO CAULIFLOWER RICE

calories: 250
fat: 22g
carbs: 5.6g
fibre: 2.2g
protein: 7g

Ingredients

- 2 cauliflower heads
- 8oz/225g asiago cheese*, shredded
- 4oz/120ml double cream

Method

1 Whizz the cauliflower in a food processor to make cauliflower rice.

2 In a large saute pan, add the riced cauliflower and 2 tbsp of water. Cover and cook for 5 minutes.

3 Add the cream and cheese and mix until cheese is melted.

4 Taste to see if the cauliflower is done.

5 Take off the heat and serve.

CHEF'S NOTE
Calcium in asiago cheese helps maintain heart rhythm and muscle function.

AVOCADO FRIES

SERVES 3

calories: 587
fat: 51g
carbs: 12g
fibre: 5g
protein: 17g

Ingredients

For the fries:
- 3 avocados
- 1 egg
- 12½oz/360g almond meal
- 12½oz/360g sunflower oil

- ¼ tsp cayenne pepper
- ½ tsp salt

For the spicy mayo:
- 2 tbsp homemade mayonnaise
- 1 tsp sriracha

Method

1 Break an egg into a bowl and beat it. In another bowl, mix your almond meal with some salt and cayenne pepper.

2 Slice each avocado in half and take out the seed. Peel off the skin off every half. and slice each avocado vertically into 4 or 5 pieces (depending on the size of the avocado).

3 Start heating your deep fryer (or deep pan with lots of oil) to about 350°F. If you don't have a cooking thermometer, try sticking a wooden spoon into the oil when it's been heating for about 7-8 minutes. If bubbles arise from the spoon, your oil is hot enough for deep frying.

4 Coat each slice of avocado in the egg. Roll each coated slice in the almond meal until covered.

5 Carefully lower each avocado slice into the deep fryer (or pan) to avoid splashing. It will hurt!

6 Allow each piece to fry from 45 seconds to a minute until a light brown. Dark brown means they've been in there a few seconds too long.

7 Transfer quickly to a plate lined with a paper towel to soak up the excess oil.

8 Mix some sriracha sauce and mayonnaise to serve as a dip.

CHEF'S NOTE
You can use coconut oil instead of sunflower oil.

FRIED CHICKEN AND STREAKY BACON PATTIES

calories: 415
fat: 23g
carbs: 4.5g
fibre: 3g
protein: 39g

Ingredients

- 4 slices streaky bacon
- 2 red peppers, seeded
- 5oz/150g chicken
- 2oz/50g grated parmesan cheese
- 3 tbsp coconut flour
- 1 egg
- 2 tbsp coconut oil
- Salt and pepper, to taste

Method

1 Cook the streaky bacon until crisp then drain on paper towels and chop well.

2 Place the peppers in a food processor and pulse until coarsely chopped.

3 Add the chicken and cooked streaky bacon then pulse until it comes together in a smooth mixture.

4 Pulse in the parmesan cheese, coconut flour, and egg then season with salt and pepper.

5 Melt the coconut oil in a large frying pan over medium-high heat.

6 Shape the mixture into 9 patties and fry for 2 to 3 minutes on each side until browned.

7 Drain on paper towels and repeat with the remaining mixture.

CHEF'S NOTE
Streaky bacon contains vitamin B-12 which is important for healthy red blood cells.

CHICKEN STRIP SLIDER

calories: 625
fat: 51g
carbs: 4.3g
fibre: 2g
protein: 34.8g

Ingredients

Almond flour buns
- 1oz/25g almond flour
- 2oz/50g flax seed
- 3 tbsp parmesan cheese
- 2 eggs
- 4 tbsp butter

- 1 tsp baking soda
- 1 tsp southwest seasoning
- 1 tsp paprika
- ½ tsp apple cider vinegar
- 4 chicken breasts

Method

1 Preheat oven to 180C/350F/GAS4.

2 Mix together all dry ingredients in a large mixing bowl.

3 Melt butter in the microwave, then add eggs, vinegar, stevia and butter to mixture.

4 Mix everything well and spread the mixture out between 8 muffin top slots in a pan.

5 Bake for 15-17 minutes. Once baked, let cool for 5 minutes, then cut buns in half.

6 Whilst the buns are baking cook the chicken breasts on a grill until cooked through.

7 Cut the cooked breast lengthways to make 8 pieces.

8 When the buns are ready place a piece of chicken in each to serve.

CHEF'S NOTE
Serve with crisy green lettuce and some BBQ sauce.

DINNERS

CHICKEN ENCHILADA CASSEROLE

calories: 406
fat: 24g
carbs: 7g
fibre: 1g
protein: 37g

Ingredients

- 1lb/450g boneless skinless chicken breasts trimmed & pounded
- 14oz/400g of enchilada sauce store bought or from scratch
- 7oz/200g finely crumbled feta cheese
- 4 green chiles, chopped
- 3 tbsp chopped fresh coriander
- Pinch of salt
- Pinch of pepper
- Olive oil spray or use olive oil in a little bowl with a brush
- 15oz/425g shredded cheddar cheese

Method

1 Preheat oven to 230C/450F/GAS8.

2 Pat the chicken dry and season with salt and pepper.

3 Combine the chicken and enchilada sauce in a medium saucepan & simmer for 15-20 minutes over medium-low heat until cooked through.

4 Remove chicken from pan and shred into bite-sized pieces. Combine shredded chicken, the enchilada sauce, feta cheese, chiles and coriander in a bowl.

5 Spray a casserole dish with olive oil (or use a brush) and coat the entire bottom and sides.

6 Evenly spread cheddar cheese on the bottom of the dish. Add the chicken mixture, then add the rest of the cheddar cheese on top.

7 Cover with foil and bake for about 10 minutes. Remove foil and bake an additional 3 to 5 minutes to melt the cheese.

CHEF'S NOTE

You can serve with lime wedges and sour cream.

ROASTED PECAN GREEN BEANS

calories: 240
fat: 20.8g
carbs: 5.3g
fibre: 2g
protein: 4.7g

Ingredients

- 8oz/225g green beans
- 2 tbsp olive oil
- 2oz/50g chopped pecans
- 2 tbsp parmesan cheese
- ½ lemon zest
- 1 tsp minced garlic
- ½ tsp red pepper Flakes

Method

1 Preheat oven to 230C/450F/GAS8,

2 Blitz the pecans in a food processor until they are roughly chopped.

3 In a large mixing bowl, mix together green beans, pecans, olive oil, parmesan cheese, the zest of ½ lemon, minced garlic, and red pepper flakes.

4 Spread everything out on a foiled baking sheet.

5 Roast the green beans in the oven for approx 20 minutes or until cooked through.

6 Let cool for 4-5 minutes, then serve!

CHEF'S NOTE

Try pairing this lovey dish with steak too.

LOW CARB KETO LASAGNA

calories: 364
fat: 21g
carbs: 12g
fibre: 7g
protein: 32g

Ingredients

- 1 tbsp butter
- 8oz/225g spicy Italian sausage
- 15oz/425g ricotta cheese
- 2 tbsp coconut flour
- 1 egg
- 1½ tsp salt
- ½ tsp pepper

- 1 tsp garlic powder
- 1 clove garlic, finely chopped
- 12½oz/360g mozzarella cheese
- 3½oz/100g parmesan cheese
- 4 courgettes quatered lengthways

- 500ml/2 cups marinara sauce
- 1 tbsp mixed Italian herb seasoning
- ½ tsp red pepper flake
- 2 tbsp chopped fresh basil

Method

1 Heat butter in a large frying pan over medium-high heat. Crumble and brown Italian sausage. Remove from heat and let cool.

2 Preheat oven to 190C/375F/GAS5 and coat a 9×9" baking dish with cooking spray or butter.

3 Add ricotta cheese, mozzarella cheese, parmesan cheese, egg, coconut flour, salt, garlic, garlic powder, and pepper to a small bowl and mix until smooth. Set aside. Add Italian seasoning and red pepper flakes to a jar of marinara, stir well. Set aside.

4 Add a layer of sliced courgette to the bottom of greased dish. Spread of cheese mixture over courgette, sprinkle with Italian sausage and then add a layer of sauce.

5 Repeat process 3-4 times until ingredients are all gone, ending with a layer of sauce. Add remaining mozzarella cheese and sprinkle with remaining parmesan cheese.

6 Cover with foil and bake for 30 minutes. Remove foil and bake for an additional 15 minutes until golden brown. Remove from oven and let sit for 5-10 minutes before serving. Sprinkle with fresh basil if desired.

CHEF'S NOTE

Marinara is a simple Italian/American sauce now widely availible in the UK.

54

KETO BUFFALO WINGS

calories: 391
fat: 33g
carbs: 1g
fibre: 0g
protein: 31g

Ingredients

- 12 chicken wings
- 4 tbsp butter
- 2oz/60ml hot sauce
- 1 clove minced garlic

- 1 tsp paprika
- 1 tsp cayenne pepper
- 1 tsp salt
- 1 tsp black pepper

Method

1 Preheat oven to 200C/400F/GAS6. Using a wire rack, with a baking dish or sheet underneath, spread wings evenly. The wire rack will keep them from getting soggy on the bottom. Rub some olive oil and season generously with salt and pepper.

2 Bake for about 45 minutes or until crispy and at 140C/275F/GAS1.

3 While your chicken wings are baking (or frying, cook whichever way you prefer), add your garlic and butter to a small saucepan over medium-low heat until hot and melted.

4 Once melted, add the rest of the ingredients and mix together.

5 When your wings are cooked, toss them in a bowl with sauce, until coated.

6 Serve with salad and celery, or coated with blue cheese crumbles.

CHEF'S NOTE

Cayenne pepper helps increase the amount of heat your body produces, making you burn more calories per day.

PORTOBELLO BUN CHEESEBURGERS

calories: 336
fat: 22.8g
carbs: 4g
fibre: 1.2g
protein: 29.g

Ingredients

- 1lb/450g grass fed minced beef
- 1 tbsp Worcestershire sauce
- 1 tsp pink Himalayan salt
- 1 tsp black pepper

- 1 tbsp avocado oil
- 8 portobello mushroom caps, destemmed, rinsed and dabbed dry
- 4 slices sharp cheddar cheese

Method

1 In a bowl, combine minced beef, Worcestershire sauce, salt, and pepper.

2 Form beef into burger patties.

3 In a large pan, heat avocado oil over medium heat. Add portobello mushroom caps and cook for about 3-4 minutes on each side. Remove from heat.

4 In the same pan, cook burger patties for 4-5 mins on either side or until cooked through.

5 Add cheese to top of burgers and cover with a lid and allow cheese to melt, about 1 minute.

6 Layer one portobello mushroom cap, then cheeseburger, desired garnishes, and top with remaining portobello mushroom cap.

CHEF'S NOTE

You can garnish with sliced dill pickles, romaine, sugar-free barbecue sauce, and spicy brown mustard.

KETO CHINESE ASPARAGUS CHICKEN STIR-FRY

calories: 240
fat: 41g
carbs: 10g
fibre: 4g
protein: 24g

Ingredients

- ¼ onion, diced
- 16 spears of asparagus, chopped
- 1 chicken breast, diced
- 4oz/120g avocado oil
- 2 tbsp gluten-free tamari sauce or coconut aminos
- 1 tsp sesame oil

Method

1 Add avocado oil to a hot frying pan or wok on a medium heat.

2 Add the diced onion and cook until it turns translucent.

3 Add in the diced chicken and stir-fry until the chicken is cooked. Set aside.

4 Then add the asparagus into the frying pan and stir-fry for 5 minutes on high heat.

5 Add the chicken back in, season with tamari sauce and sesame oil. Cook until piping hot then serve.

CHEF'S NOTE
Sesame oil is good for maintaining blood sugar levels.

LOW CARB MINI MEXICAN MEATZAS

calories: 418
fat: 24g
carbs: 5.5g
fibre: 2g
protein: 39.8g

Ingredients

- 1lb/450g minced beef
- 1 onion
- 1 egg
- 1 head cauliflower
- 2 tsp chilli powder
- 1 tsp cumin
- 1 tsp salt
- ½ tsp pepper
- 1 tsp garlic powder
- ¼ red onion, sliced thin
- 9oz/250g cheddar cheese, shredded
- 4oz/125g sweet pepper slices

Method

1 Preheat oven to 180C/350F/GAS4.

2 Add onion to a food processor and pulse until finely chopped.

3 Place in a large bowl and then add cauliflower to food processor and pulse until it looks like grains of rice.

4 Add that to the large bowl along with meat, a beaten egg, chilli powder, cumin, salt, pepper and garlic powder.

5 Mix well and split meat into 4.

6 Take each piece and make into a very thin, round pizza looking shell. Place on a lined baking tray.

7 Bake for 20 minutes or until meat is cooked.

8 Take out of the oven, sprinkle cheese and add onions and peppers on top.

9 Return to the oven until the cheese is melted.

CHEF'S NOTE
Serve with avocado slices and sliced tomatoes.

EASY STEAK FAJITA

calories: 415
fat: 27g
carbs: 5.5g
fibre: 3g
protein: 36g

Ingredients

- 2oz/60ml olive oil
- 2oz/60ml fresh lime juice
- 1 tbsp chilli powder
- 1 tsp mince cumin
- 1 tsp paprika
- 1 tsp minced garlic

- 1lb/450g beef flank steak cut into strips
- 2 tbsp coconut oil
- 1 yellow onion, sliced
- 1 red pepper, sliced
- 1 green pepper, sliced
- Salt and pepper, to taste

Method

1 Whisk together the olive oil, lime juice, chilli powder, cumin, and paprika in a bowl to make a marinade.

2 Add the garlic and red pepper flakes, stirring to combine.

3 Season the steak with salt and pepper then place it in a freezer bag and pour in the marinade.

4 Shake to coat then seal and chill for 2 to 4 hours.

5 Preheat a grill to high heat and oil the grates.

6 Add the steak strips to the grill and cook until done to the desired level then set aside.

7 Heat the coconut oil in a large frying pan over medium heat.

8 Add the peppers and onions then season with salt and pepper – sauté until they are just tender, about 5 minutes.

CHEF'S NOTE
You can add ½ tsp chilli flakes if you prefer it more spicy and serve in lettuce cups with sour cream.

SHAKE AND BAKE PORK CHOP

calories: 350
fat: 14g
carbs: 1g
fibre: 0.5g
protein: 52g

Ingredients

- 8 small boneless pork loin chops
- ½ tbsp psyllium husk powder
- ½ tsp paprika
- ½ tsp salt
- ¼ tsp garlic powder
- ¼ tsp onion powder
- ¼ tsp dried oregano

Method

1 Preheat the oven to 180C/350F/GAS4 and line a baking sheet with parchment.

2 Rinse the pork chops in cool water then pat dry.

3 Combine the psyllium husk powder and spices in a zippered freezer bag.

4 Add the pork chops one at a time and shake to coat.

5 Place the pork chops on the baking sheet and bake for 20-30 or until cooked through.

CHEF'S NOTE
Psyllium is a soluble fibre particulalry good for gut health

EASY COCONUT CHICKEN

calories: 286
fat: 20g
carbs: 3g
fibre: 0g
protein: 23g

Ingredients

- 1 tbsp coconut oil
- 5 cloves garlic, crushed
- 4 tbsp apple cider vinegar
- 1lb/450g boneless skinless, chicken thighs cut into bite sizes pieces
- ½ tsp black pepper
- ½ tsp Sea Salt
- 2oz/60ml water
- 250ml/1 cup tinned coconut milk

Method

1 In a sauce pan over medium/low heat add the coconut oil and diced chicken thighs.

2 Cook for 2 -3 minutes and then add the apple cider vinegar, water and garlic cloves and cook for 3 minutes.

3 Add the black pepper and Sea Salt and cook until the liquid all boils down. This should take roughly 10 minutes.

4 Stir in the coconut milk and simmer for 5 to 10 minutes until your liquid thickens slightly and you have a gravy.

CHEF'S NOTE
Serve with cauliflower rice or courgette noodles.

LOW CARB MEATBALLS ITALIAN STYLE

calories: 204
fat: 14g
carbs: 4g
fibre: 2g
protein: 16g

Ingredients

- 1lb/450g minced beef
- 2oz/50g grated parmesan cheese
- 2oz/50g golden flaxseed meal
- 1 tbsp Italian seasoning
- ¾ tsp sea salt
- ½ tsp black pepper
- 2oz/60ml unsweetened coconut milk

- 1 onion, finely chopped
- 1 egg
- 3 cloves garlic, minced
- 2 tbsp fresh parsley, chopped
- 250ml/1 cup tomato passata/sieved tomatoes

Method

1 Preheat the oven to 220C/425F/GAS7. Line a baking sheet with parchment paper.

2 In a large bowl, stir together the grated Parmesan cheese, golden flaxseed meal, Italian seasoning, sea salt, and black pepper.

3 Whisk in the milk, onion, egg, garlic, and fresh parsley. Let the mixture sit for a couple of minutes.

4 Mix in the minced beef using your hands, until just incorporated. (Don't over-mix to avoid tough meatballs.

5 Form the mixture into 1-inch balls and place on the lined baking sheet. (don't pack the meatballs too tightly).

6 Bake for 10-12 minutes, or until the meatballs are cooked through.

7 Meanwhile warm the passata through in a pan. Add the cooked meatballs and cook until pipting hot.

8 Garnish with additional fresh parsley and serve.

CHEF'S NOTE
This is good served with courgette noodles.

ASPARAGUS STUFFED CHICKEN PARMESAN

calories: 317
fat: 26g
carbs: 11g
fibre: 4g
protein: 23g

Ingredients

- 3 chicken breasts
- 1 tsp garlic paste
- 12 stalks asparagus, stalks removed
- 4oz/125g cream cheese
- 1 tbsp butter
- 1 tsp olive oil
- 125ml/½ cup tomato passata/sieved tomatoes
- 9oz/250g shredded mozzarella
- Salt and pepper, to taste

Method

1 Butterfly the chicken (slice it in half without slicing it all the way through. The chicken breast should open out like a butterfly with one end still intact in the middle).

2 Remove the hardy stalks of the asparagus and set aside.

3 Rub salt, pepper and garlic paste all over the chicken breasts (inside and outside).

4 Divide cream cheese between the chicken breasts and spread it on the inside. Place four stalks of asparagus and then fold one side of the breast over the other, tucking it in place with a toothpick to make sure it doesn't come open.

5 Preheat the oven and set it to grill. Add butter and olive oil to a hot frying pan and place the chicken

breasts in it. Cook the breasts on each side for 6-7 minutes unti the chicken is cooked through.

6 Meanwhile pre heat the grill.

7 Top each breast with passata sauce and divide the shredded mozzarella on top. Place under the grill until the cheese melts.

CHEF'S NOTE
Cooking times may slightly differ depending on the size of the chicken breast.

63

SAUSAGE AND EGG MEATLOAF PIE

calories: 408
fat: 29g
carbs: 1g
fibre: 0g
protein: 34g

Ingredients

- 1lb/450g mince pork
- 15oz/425g shredded mozzarella cheese
- 6 eggs
- 1 tsp mixed herbs
- Large pinch salt & pepper

Method

1 Preheat oven to 180C/350F/GAS4.

2 Brown the pork mince..

3 Whisk together eggs, seasonings and shredded cheese.

4 Drain the pork and allow to cool.

5 Blend the pork and egg mixture and pour into a 9" pie pan.

6 Bake for 45-55 minutes or until firm and cooked through.

CHEF'S NOTE
This simple meatloaf style dish is great served with steamed broccoli.

SOUPS & SALADS

LOW-CARB PUMPKIN SOUP WITH CHORIZO CRUMB

calories: 254
fat: 18.9g
carbs: 9.1g
fibre: 1.4g
protein: 12.7g

Ingredients

- 2 tbsp virgin coconut oil
- 1 brown onion, chopped
- 1lb/450g chopped pumpkin
- 1 garlic clove, minced
- 1 tbsp fresh grated ginger
- Pinch of garam masala

- ½ tsp cumin
- ½ tsp paprika
- 1.5l/6 cups chicken stock
- 1 Mexican chorizo sausage
- Salt and pepper, to taste

Method

1 Place the stock in a pan on a medium heat and simmer for 10 minutes until the stock reduces in volume by about a third.

2 Preheat the oven to 180C/350F/GAS4.

3 Slice the pumpkin in half, remove the seeds and peel. Cut into cubes, toss in a little olive oil, bake for 20 -25 mins in the oven until tender and then set aside.

4 Meanwhile, heat the coconut oil in a pan on a medium heat. Peel and finely chop the onion and garlic. Gently fry the onion on a medium heat for 3 mins until soft. Add the garlic and fry together for 1 further minute.

5 Add the cumin, ginger, garam masala, paprika, salt and pepper to the onions and garlic and fry for 4 minutes on a medium-low heat.

6 Add the roasted pumpkin and concentrated stock. Simmer on a medium heat for about 5 minutes. Place in a high-speed blender and process until smooth. Add a little more stock or water if needed to reach your desired consistency.

7 Remove the skin from the chorizo sausage. Finely dice the chorizo meat and fry on a medium heat in a dry non-stick pan for about 5 minutes until cooked through and crispy.

8 Ladle the pumpkin soup into bowls, top with the chorizo crumb and optionally, top with yoghurt, sesame seeds and watercress.

SLOW COOKER PUMPKIN & COCONUT SOUP

calories: 234
fat: 21.7g
carbs: 11.4g
fibre: 1.5g
protein: 2.3g

Ingredients

- 1 onion, diced
- 1 tsp fresh ginger, grated
- 1 tsp garlic, crushed
- 2 tbsp butter
- 1lb 2oz/500g pumpkin chunks
- 750ml/3 cups vegetable stock
- 500ml/2 cups coconut milk
- Salt and pepper, to taste

Method

1 Place all the ingredients into slow cooker dish and combine.

2 Cook on HIGH for 4-6 hours OR Cook on LOW for 6-8 hours.

3 Puree until smooth using a stick/immersion blender.

4 Check the seasoning and serve.

CHEF'S NOTE

You can also cook on stove top for 30 - 45 mins.

KETO PHO STYLE CHICKEN SOUP

calories: 152
fat: 7.2g
carbs: 6.6g
fibre: 5.2g
protein: 17.4g

Ingredients

- 4 chicken thighs , boneless
- 1 garlic cloe, crushed
- 1 fresh ginger root
- 1 onion
- 2 tbsp fish sauce
- 1.5 litre/6 cups chicken stock
- 300g/11oz shirataki noodles

Method

1 Peel ginger and cut into large chunks.

2 Slice the onion.

3 Add chicken stock, garlic, fish sauce & chicken thighs. Reduce heat and simmer for 20-30 mins until the chicken is tender.

4 Remove chicken and discard ginger root chunks. Let chicken cool until you can shred it. You can discard the skin or shred it to up too.

5 Return shredded chicken to soup along with the noodles. Warm through and serve.

CHEF'S NOTE
Shiritaki noodles (also called Miracle noodles) are very low carb.

KETO BROCCOLI SOUP WITH TURMERIC & GINGER

calories: 439
fat: 36g
carbs: 17g
fibre: 4g
protein: 8g

Ingredients

- 1 onion
- 3 cloves garlic
- 500ml/2 cups coconut milk
- 1 tsp salt

- 1 tsp turmeric powder
- 2 tsp fresh ginger, chopped
- 2 broccoli heads, chopped into florets
- 500ml/2 cups vegetable stock

Method

1 Pour half of the coconut milk in a pan and place on low heat.

2 Add the onion and garlic and cook for 5 minutes until soft.

3 Once cooked, add the salt, turmeric, ginger, broccoli florets, stock and remaining coconut milk.

4 Simmer for 20 mins, stirring occasionally and mashing the broccoli.

5 Let the mixture cool, before placing in a food processor and blending into a puree.

CHEF'S NOTE

You can serve with yoghurt, roasted almonds, fresh greens and sesame seeds.

TACO SOUP CROCKPOT

calories: 505
fat: 32g
carbs: 8.5g
fibre: 0g
protein: 44g

Ingredients

- 900g/2lb lean minced beef
- 450g/16oz cream cheese
- 15oz/425g diced tomatoes
- 3 tbsp taco seasoning

- 1.5 litre/6 cups chicken broth
- 4oz/125g shredded cheddar cheese
- 2oz/60ml sour cream

Method

1 Brown the minced beef in a large saucepan until cooked through then drain the fat off and add the meat to the slow cooker.

2 Sprinkle in the chopped cream cheese along with the diced tomatoes and taco seasoning.

3 Pour in the chicken broth then cover and cook on low heat for 4 hours or on high for 2 hours.

4 Stir everything together then adjust seasoning with salt and pepper to taste.

5 Spoon into bowls and serve with shredded cheese and sour cream.

CHEF'S NOTE
Riboflavin in sour cream has antioxidant properties which help fight free radical damages in the body.

KETO GREEK MEATBALLS SALAD

calories: 399
fat: 36g
carbs: 2g
fibre: 0g
protein: 20g

Ingredients

For the meatballs
- 1lb/450g minced lamb or beef
- 2 tsp dried oregano
- 2 tbsp fresh mint, finely chopped
- 2 cloves garlic, peeled and crushed
- Salt and pepper, to taste

- 4 tbsp olive oil

For the salad
- 1 tomato, cut into wedges
- Few lettuce leaves, to serve with
- 1 lemon, cut into wedges
- 4 tbsp flat leaf parsley, chopped

Method

1 Preheat oven to 180C/350F/GAS4.

2 Mix the mince lamb with the dried oregano, mint, garlic, salt and pepper. Form small meatballs from the mixture.

3 Add olive oil to a large pan and fry the meatballs in batches until browned. Transfer to a lined baking tray and bake in the oven for 10 minutes to ensure the centre of the meatballs cook through.

4 Serve the meatballs over a salad made of lettuce and tomato wedges. Generously squeeze over the lemon and garnish the salad with chopped parsley.

CHEF'S NOTE
Lemon helps balance your body's pH and optimise overall health.

BLTA PESTO CHICKEN SALAD

calories: 375
fat: 27g
carbs: 3g
fibre: 0g
protein: 27g

Ingredients

- 1lb/450g chicken, cooked and cubed
- 6 slices streaky bacon
- 1 avocado, cubed
- 10 vine ripened tomatoes, quartered

- 4oz/125g mayonnaise
- 2 tbsp green pesto
- 1 red onion, sliced
- 1 romaine lettuce, shredded

Method

1 Cook the bacon until very crisp. When it cools crumble into small pieces.

2 In a large mixing bowl, combine together the chicken, streaky bacon pieces, avocado, tomatoes, mayonnaise, lettuce, red onion and pesto.

3 Toss gently to coat well. Loosen with a little olove oil if needed.

4 Check the seasoning and serve.

CHEF'S NOTE
Feel free to add some cubed cucumber and spinach leaves to this salad too.

STEAK & CHIMICHURRI SALAD

calories: 438
fat: 32g
carbs: 7g
fibre: 2g
protein: 30g

Ingredients

- 1 romaine lettuce, shredded
- ¼ head red cabbage, shredded
- 2 radishes, sliced thinly
- 2 tbsp fresh coriander, coarsely chopped

- 1 tbsp house vinaigrette salad dressing
- 3 tbsps Chimichurri Sauce
- 4oz/125g great steak

Method

1 Toss the first five ingredients together with House Vinaigrette.

2 Flash fry your steak until cooked to your perference (medium rare is best)

3 Thinly slice the steak and serve with the salad and the Chimichurri Sauce. on the side.

CHEF'S NOTE

Chimichurri sauce is an Argentinian sauce which is readily availble in US & UK supermarkets.

LOADED CHICKEN SALAD

calories: 430
fat: 29.36g
carbs: 12.86g
fibre: 6.12g
protein: 31.73g

Ingredients

- 4 boneless chicken breasts,
- 1 tbsp extra virgin olive oil
- ¼ tsp Himalayan salt
- ¼ tsp black pepper
- 1 avocado
- 3½oz/100g mozzarella balls
- 1 tomato

- 1 jar artichoke hearts, chopped
- ½ red onion
- 4 asparagus spears
- 20 leaves basil
- 200g/7oz baby spinach

Dressing
- 2 tbsp extra virgin olive oil
- 1½ tbsp balsamic vinegar
- 1 tsp dijon mustard
- 1 clove garlic
- Pinch Himalayan salt
- Pinch black pepper

Method

1 Peel and dice the avocado. Slice the red onion. Dice the tomato. Pile the basil leaves together, roll them up and slice. Cut the stems off the asparagus and slice in half. Crush the garlic.

2 Slice the chicken breasts in half lengthwise. Sprinkle salt and pepper on each side. Heat the 1 tbsp of olive oil in a cast iron frying pan and place the chicken breasts in. Fry on each side, about 3 until they have a nice golden brown colour and are cooked through. Add the asparagus beside the chicken breasts and cook a few minutes until soft and grilled. Take out the chicken and slice.

3 In a small bowl, combine the crushed garlic, olive oil, balsamic vinegar, dijon, and salt & peper.

4 Add the baby spinach to plates.

5 Pile the grilled chicken, avocado, mozzarella, tomatoes, artichoke, red onions, asparagus and basil leaves on top. Pour the dressing over and serve.

CHEF'S NOTE
Sundried tomatoes could be used in place of artichokes if you prefer.

KETO CEASAR SALAD

calories: 527
fat: 22.75g
carbs: 1.8g
fibre: 0.5g
protein: 13g

Ingredients

- 1 egg yolk
- 2 tbsp avocado oil
- 1 tbsp apple cider vinegar
- 1 tsp dijion mustard
- 4 anchovy filets, finely chopped

- 2 garlic cloves
- 1 tbsp grated parmesan
- 1 romain lettuce shredded
- 2oz/50g crispy bacon, chopped
- 1 tbsp parmesan, shavings

Method

1 Create a mayonnaise by gently blending together the egg yolk, apple cider, mustard, vinegar and avocado oil.

2 Once the base mayo is ready add the anchovies, garlic and grated parmesan to the cup.

3 Blend slowly until all ingredients are well blended together and create a smooth mayonnaise-like dressing.

4 Lay the lettuce out on a plate and drizzle the dressing over the top.

5 Sprinkle the bacon pieces over and garnish with the shaved parmesan.

CHEF'S NOTE
Add chicken and prawns if you wish to this tasty salad.

SHRIMP AVOCADO SALAD

calories: 255
fat: 13g
carbs: 4g
fibre: 1g
protein: 27g

Ingredients

- 1lb/450g cooked shrimp (peeled and deveined)
- 2oz/60ml fresh lime juice
- 1 tsp olive oil
- Salt and pepper

- 1 avocado, pitted and diced
- 1 small tomato, diced
- 2oz/50g red onion, diced
- 2 tbsp fresh chopped coriander

Method

1 Chop the shrimp into bite-sized pieces.

2 Whisk together the lime juice, olive oil, salt, and pepper in a bowl.

3 Toss in the shrimp, avocado, tomato, red onion, and coriander.

4 When well combined, cover and chill until ready to serve.

CHEF'S NOTE
You can add 1 jalapeno (seeded and minced) if you like.

SAUCES & SEASONING

ENCHILADA SAUCE

calories: 53
fat: 2g
carbs: 2g
fibre: 0g
protein: 2g

Ingredients

- 500ml/2 cups tomato passata/ sieved tomatoes
- 1 chicken stock cube
- 3 tbsp tomato puree
- 1 bay leaf
- 2 tbsp mild chilli powder

- 1 tbsp sweet paprika
- 2 tsp ground cumin
- 1 tsp dried oregano
- ½ tsp salt
- ½ tsp granulated garlic
- ½ tsp onion powder

- ¼ tsp instant coffee powder
- Pinch ground clove
- Pinch ground cinnamon

Method

1 Put all of the ingredients into a medium to large frying pan on medium heat.

2 Simmer gently for 20 minutes, stirring occasionally, until the r sauce has reduced a little.

3 The sauce will be thin but flavorful.

4 It will thicken-up in the oven as the enchiladas cook..

CHEF'S NOTE
Add a ltitle sweetener if the sauce is a bitter, it will help balance the flavours. Discard the bay leaf before using.

HOMEMADE WORCESTERSHIRE SAUCE

calories: 10
fat: 0.1g
carbs: 1.6g
fibre: 0g
protein: 1g

Ingredients

- 4oz/125g apple cider vinegar
- 2 tbsp water
- 2 tbsp soy sauce
- 1 tbsp brown sugar
- 1 tsp mustard powder
- ¼ tsp onion powder
- ¼ tsp garlic powder
- ¼ tsp mince cinnamon
- Mince black pepper, to taste

Method

1 Combine apple cider vinegar, water, soy sauce, brown sugar, mustard powder, onion powder, garlic powder, mince cinnamon, and black pepper together in a saucepan.

2 Bring to a boil and cook until fragrant, about 45 seconds.

3 Cool to room temperature and store in the fridge.

CHEF'S NOTE
Sodium plays an important role in the removal of any excess carbon dioxide that has accumulated in the body.

HOMEMADE KETO MAYONNAISE

calories: 95
fat: 11g
carbs: 0g
fibre: 0g
protein: 0g

Ingredients

- 4 egg yolk
- 12 tbsp apple cider vinegar
- 2 lemons, juiced
- 2 tsp sea salt

- 1 tsp paprika
- 1 tsp garlic powder
- 2 tbsp avocado oil

Method

1 Gently blend together the egg yolk, apple cider vinegar, lemon juice, sea salt, paprika and garlic powder

2 Add the avocado oil to emulsify.

3 transfer to a clean jar to store.

CHEF'S NOTE
You can refrigerate and keep for up to 2 weeks.

SOUTHWESTERN SEASONING MIX

calories: 2
fat: 0g
carbs: 0g
fibre: 0g
protein: 0g

Ingredients

- 2oz/50g chilli powder
- 2oz/50g onion powder
- 2 tbsp ground cumin
- 2 tbsp ground coriander
- 2 tbsp dried oregano
- 2 tbsp dried basil
- 1 tbsp dried thyme
- 1 tbsp garlic powder

Method

1 lay all your dry ingredients out.

2 Add each in turn to a pestle and mortar and grind together to form a combined powder.

3 Adjust the seasonign to suit your taste.

CHEF'S NOTE

Store in an airtight container. Use as a seasoning for cooked vegetables, grilled meats or chip dips.

MARINARA SAUCE

calories: 159
fat: 10.5g
carbs: 10.7g
fibre: 3g
protein: 2g

Ingredients

- 2 tbsp of olive oil
- 1 clove of garlic, crushed
- 2 tsp of onion flakes
- 2 tsp fresh thyme, finely chopped
- 2 tsp fresh oregano, finely chopped
- 1 tsp each salt & pepper

- 1lt/4 cups tomato passata/sieved tomatoes
- 2 tsp erythritol
- 1 tsp salt
- 1 tsp red wine vinegar
- 2 tbsp fresh parsley, finely chopped

Method

1 In a saucepan, place the oil, garlic, onion flakes, thyme and oregano. Saute over medium heat for 3 minutes.

2 Add the tomato passata and stir well.

3 Add the erythritol, pepper, salt and red wine vinegar and bring to a simmer.

4 Turn off the heat and stir through the parsley.

5 Cool the sauce.

CHEF'S NOTE
Scoop into an airtight jar and store in fridge.

DESSETS
SNACKS &
SMOOTHIES

EASY KETO CHOCOLATE MOUSSE

calories: 227
fat: 24g
carbs: 3g
fibre: 1.5g
protein: 4g

Ingredients

- 2oz/60ml unsalted butter
- 2oz/50g cream cheese
- 3oz/75g double cream, whipped
- 1 tbsp cocoa powder
- Stevia, to taste

Method

1 Soften butter and combine with sweetener, stirring until completely blended.

2 Add cream cheese; blend until smooth.

3 Add cocoa powder and blend completely.

4 Whip double cream and gradually add to the mixture.

5 Spoon into small glasses and refrigerate for 30 minutes.

CHEF'S NOTE
For extra smoothness add coconut oil.

COCONUT DROP SCONES

calories: 280
fat: 16g
carbs: 3.5g
fibre: 1g
protein: 8g

Ingredients

- 2 eggs
- 2oz/50g cream cheese
- 1 tbsp almond flour
- 1 tsp cinnamon
- ½ tbsp erythritol
- 1 pinch salt
- 2oz/50g unsweetened shredded coconut
- 2 tbsp sugar free Maple Syrup

Method

1 Crack the eggs into a mixing bowl and whisk.

2 Add in cream cheese and whisk until completely combined and creamy.

3 Whisk in the almond flour, cinnamon, erythritol and salt to complete the scone mixture.

4 On a pan on medium heat, add in half the drop scone batter. Cook until the edges start to brown and look dry (about 3-5 minutes). Flip carefully and cook the other side for up to a minute.

5 Transfer the drop scones onto a plate and sprinkle with the shredded coconut.

6 Drizzle with maple syrup to serve.

CHEF'S NOTE
Make sure your heat is not too high, otherwise the drop scone will burn before the centre cooks.

ALMOND LEMON CAKE SANDWICHES

calories: 180
fat: 17.5g
carbs: 1g
fibre: 0.8g
protein: 2.8g

Ingredients

Almond Lemon Cakes
- 4oz/125g almond flour
- 4oz/125g coconut flour
- 4oz/120ml butter
- 3 eggs
- 4oz/125g erythritol
- 1 tbsp lemon juice

- 1 tbsp coconut milk
- 1 tsp cinnamon
- ½ tsp almond extract
- ½ tsp vanilla extract
- ½ tsp baking soda
- ½ tsp apple cider vinegar
- ¼ tsp liquid stevia

- ¼ tsp salt

Sandwich icing
- 2oz/50g powdered erythritol
- 4oz/120g cream cheese
- 4 tbsp butter
- 2 tbsp double cream

Method

1 Preheat your oven to 170C/325F/GAS3.

2 Sift and mix the coconut flour, almond flour, cinnamon salt, and baking soda.

3 Combine eggs, erythritol, vanilla extract, almond extract, lemon juice, melted butter, coconut milk, vinegar, stevia, and food colouring.

4 Mix the wet ingredients into the dry ingredients, using a hand mixer until it is fluffy.

5 Divide batter between muffin top pan and bake for 17-18 minutes or until cooked.

6 Remove from the oven and cool on a cooling rack for 10 minutes.

7 Slice cakes in half and fry them in butter until crisped. Allow to cool on the rack again.

8 Mix together the butter, cream cheese, double cream, and erythritol until fluffy.

9 Divide icing in between middle of the cakes and make a sandwich.

10 Garnish with lemon zest and pistachios.

CHEF'S NOTE
Lemon zest contain limonene, which protects against skin cancer.

SMOKED SALMON EGG STUFFED AVOCADOS

calories: 480
fat: 39g
carbs: 18g
fibre: 14g
protein: 20g

Ingredients

- 4 avocados
- 8 slices smoked salmon
- 8 eggs
- Salt

- Black pepper
- Chilli flakes
- Fresh dill

Method

1 Preheat oven to 220C/425F/GAS7.

2 Halve the avocados, remove the seed. If the hole looks small, scoop out a small bit at a time until it can hold an egg.

3 Arrange the avocado halves on a baking tray and line the hollows with strips of smoked salmon. Crack each of the eggs into a small bowl, then spoon the yolks and however much white the avocado will hold.

4 Add salt and fresh cracked black pepper on top of the eggs, to taste.

5 Gently place the baking tray in the oven and bake for about 15-20 minutes.

6 Sprinkle chilli flakes and fresh dill on top.

7 Serve warm.

CHEF'S NOTE
Avocados are a great source of vitamins C, E, K, and B-6, as well as riboflavin, niacin, folate, pantothenic acid, magnesium, and potassium.

SALTED CARAMEL CASHEW SMOOTHIE

calories: 181
fat: 19g
carbs: 1g
fibre: 0g
protein: 2g

Ingredients

- 8½oz/250ml unsweetened cashew milk
- 3 tbsp double cream
- 5 ice cubes
- 2 tbsp sugar-free salted caramel syrup
- Pinch of nutmeg to garnish

Method

1 Put all the ingredients, except the nutmeg, into a blender.

2 Blend until smooth.

3 Pour into a glass to serve and sprinkle with nutmeg.

CHEF'S NOTE
Almong milk also makes a good base for this smoothie.

KETO HUMMUS WITH CAULIFLOWER & TAHINI

calories: 124
fat: 11g
carbs: 4g
fibre: 2g
protein: 2g

Ingredients

- ½ head of cauliflower, broken into florets
- 1 tbsp olive oil
- 2 tbsp mayo
- 3 cloves of garlic, peeled
- 2 tbsp lemon juice
- 1 tbsp white tahini
- Sea salt and freshly mince black pepper, to taste
- 1 tsp fresh parsley, finely chopped for garnish

Method

1 Steam the cauliflower until softened. Drain the water well.

2 Place into a blender and blend really well with the rest of the ingredients (except for the parsley).

3 Drizzle with a little more olive oil and garnish with chopped parsley.

4 Serve with vegetable sticks like carrot or celery sticks.

CHEF'S NOTE

Take the time to blend your ingredients well, so the end result is nice and smooth.

TURKEY BANGER FRITTATA

calories: 240
fat: 16.7g
carbs: 5.5g
fibre: 0g
protein: 16.7g

Ingredients

- 12oz/350g turkey mince
- 2 peppers
- 12 eggs
- 8oz/225g sour cream

- 1 tsp pink Himalayan salt
- 1 tsp black pepper
- 2 tsp kerry gold butter

Method

1 Preheat your oven to 180C/350F/GAS4.

2 Crack all your eggs into a blender, add in the sour cream, salt and pepper. Blend on high for 30 seconds. Set aside.

3 Heat a large oven proof frying pan on medium heat. When it comes to temperature add in the butter.

4 Slice your peppers into strips. Add it to the frying pan. Sauté until browned and tender. Remove the peppers from the frying pan.

5 Add the turkey mince to the pan and cook until browned.

6 Flatten the turkey to the bottom of the frying pan. Add the peppers over it, evenly distributed. Pour the egg mix over everything.

7 Place the frying pan in the oven and bake for 30 mins until cooked thorough.

8 Cut into wedges to serve.

CHEF'S NOTE
If you want to add cheese, sprinkle over as soon as it's out of the oven

TACO TARTLETS

calories: 241
fat: 19.4g
carbs: 1.7g
fibre: 0g
protein: 13.1g

Ingredients

For the pastry:
- 8½oz blanched almond flour
- 3 tbsp coconut flour
- 5 tbsp butter
- ¼ tsp salt
- 1 tsp xanthan gum
- 1 tsp oregano

- Pinch of paprika & cayenne

For the filling:
- 2½oz/60g cheese
- 400g/14oz minced beef
- 3oz/75g mushroom
- 3 spring onions
- 2 tbsp tomato paste

- 1 tbsp olive oil
- 2 each tsp mustard & garlic
- 1 tsp each cumin & salt
- 1 tsp worcestershire
- ¼ tsp each cinnamon & pepper

Method

1 Combine all the dry ingredients of the pastry and put them into a food processor.

2 Chop cold butter into small squares and add it to your food processor. Pulse the dough together until crumbly, adding 1 tbsp of ice water until pliable.

3 Chill your dough in the freezer for 10 mins.

4 Roll the dough out between 2 pieces of clingfilm using a rolling pin. Cut out circles using a cookie cutter or a glass.

5 Put the dough pieces into your a muffin trays to make tartlets.

6 Put the oven on to heat to 170C/325F/GAS3.

7 Prepare all the filling ingredients by chopping the spring onions, mince garlic, and slice mushrooms.

8 Saute the onions and garlic in olive oil. Add minced beef to the mixture and sear it well – adding the dry spices and Worcestershire.

9 Add mushrooms and mix together. Then add tomato paste and mustard right before finishing.

10 Spoon minced beef mixture evenly into the pastry tartlets. Cover with cheese and bake for 20-25 minutes.

11 Allow to cool a little and remove the pastries to serve.

PUMPKIN CHEESECAKE BARS

calories: 273
fat: 25g
carbs: 5g
fibre: 1g
protein: 4g

Ingredients

For the crust:
- 14oz/400ml whole pecans
- 1 tsp cinnamon
- 1 tbsp coconut oil
- 12 drops liquid stevia
- 1 pinch sea salt
- For the filling:

- 8oz/225g cream cheese
- 2oz/60ml double cream
- 10oz/275g pumpkin puree
- 2 tsp vanilla extract
- 20 drops liquid stevia
- Pinch of nutmeg
- 1 tsp cinnamon

- 1 pinch salt
- 2 eggs
For the icing:
- 2oz/50g cream cheese
- 2 tbsp double cream
- 2oz/50g erythritol
- ½ tsp vanilla extract

Method

1 Preheat the oven to 180C/350F/GAS4. Combine all the crust ingredients in a food processor and pulse until the pecans are a fine crumb texture.

2 Line a 9 x 6 inch baking dish with parchment paper, letting two sides spill over for easy removal. Press the crust into the dish, making one even layer. Bake for 12 minutes, then let cool.

3 Make the filling by beating in the cream cheese and double cream until fully combined.

4 Add in the pumpkin puree, vanilla extract and liquid stevia and combine.

5 Add in the nutmeg, cinnamon and a pinch of salt then combine.

6 Add in one egg at a time, incorporating each before adding another to make a batter.

7 Once the crust has cooled a bit, pour the pumpkin cheesecake batter into the baking dish. Reduce the heat in the oven to 325°F and bake for 25-30 minutes. The middle of the pumpkin cheesecake should be a bit wobbly after baking. Refrigerate for 6 hours or, ideally, overnight.

8 To make the icing, combine all the icing ingredients and beat with an electric hand mixer until light and fluffy.

9 Frost the top of the cheesecake bars or add a dollop to each one after slicing.

KETO CHEESECAKE STUFFED BROWNIES

calories: 144
fat: 13g
carbs: 4g
fibre: 2g
protein: 4g

Ingredients

For the Filling
- 8oz/225g cream cheese
- 2oz/50g granulated erythritol
- 1 egg

For the Brownie
- 3oz/75ml low carb milk chocolate

- 5 tbsp butter
- 3 eggs
- 4oz/125g granulated erythritol
- 2oz/50g cocoa powder
- 4oz/120g almond flour

Method

1 Heat oven to 180C/350F/GAS4 and line a brownie pan with parchment. Make the cheesecake filling first by beating softened cream cheese, egg for the filling, and granulated sweetener smooth. Set aside.

2 Melt the chocolate and butter at 30-second intervals in the microwave, frequently stirring until smooth. Let cool slightly while you prepare the brownie.

3 Beat remaining eggs and sweetener on medium until the mixture is frothy.

4 Sift in the cocoa powder and almond flour and continue to beat until thin batter forms.

5 Pour in melted chocolate and beat with the hand mixer on low for 10 seconds. The batter will thicken to a mousse-like consistency.

6 Pour ¾ of the batter in the prepared pan, top with dollops of the cream cheese, then finish with the remaining brownie batter.

7 Using a spatula, smooth the batter over the cheesecake filling in a swirling pattern.

8 Bake for 25-30 minutes or until the centre is mostly set. It may jiggle slightly but once you remove it from the oven it should firm completely. Cool before slicing!

CHEF'S NOTE

Temperatures and cook times varies depending on oven. Watch these carefully and bake them until they are firm on the edges but just slightly soft at the centre.

EASY ALMOND BUTTER FUDGE

calories: 120
fat: 11g
carbs: 2.5g
fibre: 1g
protein: 3.5g

Ingredients

- 8oz/225g cream cheese, softened
- 8½oz/250ml butter, softened
- 8½oz/250ml natural almond butter (softened)
- 9oz/250g powdered erythritol
- 4oz/120g almond flour
- Liquid stevia extract, to taste

Method

1 Line a square 9x9-inch baking pan with foil or parchment paper.

2 Melt the cream cheese and butter in a small saucepan over medium heat.

3 Stir in the almond butter and cook until it melts.

4 Remove from heat then stir in the powdered erythritol and peanut flour.

5 Adjust sweetness to taste with liquid stevia extract and stir smooth.

6 Spread the mixture in the prepared baking pan as evenly as possible.

7 Chill until set then cut into squares to serve.

CHEF'S NOTE

Do not overheat the cream cheese and butter mixture. Heat in small intervals until you can mix the two together and then remove from the heat.

PECAN SOFTIES WITH SEA SALT & DARK CHOCOLATE

calories: 128
fat: 13g
carbs: 4.43g
fibre 2.16g
protein: 2.7g

Ingredients

- 4oz/120g almond flour
- 9oz/250g pecan halves
- 1½ tbsp butter, melted
- 1 tsp baking powder

- 2oz/50g erythritol
- ½ tsp sea salt
- 1 egg white
- 1oz/25g low-carb dark chocolate, melted

Method

1 Heat oven to 180C/350F/GAS4 and line a baking tray with parchment paper.

2 Combine the dry ingredients in a blender or food processor and pulse until the pecans are a coarse mince.

3 Add the butter, salt, and egg white into the blender and pulse a few times to combine. The cookie dough should like wet and feel sticky but still chunky.

4 Using a spoon or small scoop, portion out 10 rounded cookie dough balls onto the parchment. Flatten the tops of the balls until you have evenly round, flat biscuits.

5 Bake for 15 minutes or until the edges begin to brown.

6 Melt the chocolate by placing in a microwave safe bowl for 45 seconds. Stop it every 15-20 seconds to stir.

7 Drizzle each cookie with chocolate and sprinkle with extra sea salt.

CHEF'S NOTE

You can pack in a plastic container and store in the freezer.

PECAN SOFTIES WITH SEA SALT & DARK CHOCOLATE

MAKES 10

Ingredients

Method